STABAT MATER

STABAT MATER

Noble Icon of the Outcast and the Poor

Peter Daino, SM

ALBA · HOUSE   NEW · YORK

SOCIETY OF ST. PAUL, 2187 VICTORY BLVD., STATEN ISLAND, NEW YORK 10314

Library of Congress Cataloging-in-Publication Data

Daino, Peter.
  Stabat Mater.

  1. Mary, Blessed Virgin, Saint.   I. Title.
BT602.D35   1988   232.91   87-30633
ISBN 0-8189-0526-3

Designed, printed and bound in the United States of
America by the Fathers and Brothers of the
Society of St. Paul, 2187 Victory Boulevard,
Staten Island, New York 10314, as part of their
communications apostolate.

1 2 3 4 5 6 7 8 9 (Current Printing: first digit)

TABLE OF CONTENTS

DEDICATION

This book is dedicated to my mother and father
and to my whole family through whom I received the faith
which sustains and nourishes me.

Noble Icon of the Outcast and the Poor

1

A CHANGING
RELATIONSHIP

The Significance Of Mary

THE STRUGGLE for social justice is often depicted in a somber, almost gloomy manner. Reading certain authors we feel the awful weight of a nearly impossible task. This stoic-like experience of the struggle, however, does not seem to be shared by many of those who are the victims of social injustice. Among the poor in Nairobi, Kenya, for example, there is a tangible and contagious enthusiasm. Call it hope. It is a brave (perhaps humanly unfounded) conviction that things are going to get better.

I did not understand this brave-joy until I became a Marianist. In my first three years as a member of the Society of Mary I was determined to force Mary to fit into my own understanding of Christianity as a stoic sacrificial enterprise that benefits the poor and downtrodden. To my surprise she, instead, fit me

3

into her understanding or, rather, she became a way to understand what it means to be poor and downtrodden.

The deeper I enter into Marian spirituality, the more I discover that stoicism is less important than humor, sacrifice is less important than gift and that faith is what I lack most in the struggle for justice.

Mary did not write about social injustice or present her views about its eradication. She was a poor woman who proclaimed a song of victory we now call the Magnificat, stating simply that the lowly have been raised up and the hungry have been fed. It was not an ideological, economic necessity but an act of faith in the Lord of history, the Lord who has already overcome the world.

This act of faith, I think, is what lies behind the tangible and contagious enthusiasm of poor people in Nairobi.

Dietrich Bonhoeffer and others in the German Confessing Church, which resisted the inhumanity of Nazism, spoke of the "already and not yet" experience of God's Kingdom. In recent years those working for social justice have made all too clear the reality of the "not yet".

I would like to suggest that Mary, as one of the oppressed, might help us experience the "already" of God's Kingdom which is just as real as the "not yet" and just as important if we are to know the Kingdom as Jesus described it.

This book will explore the significance of Mary for the poor, the homeless, the rejected and the oppressed. It will concentrate especially on two groups of people: urban squatters and refugees. The *first* are tempted with the seduction of poverty, and to them

Mary holds out the promise of social change. The *second* are tempted with the seduction of exile, and to them Mary offers hospitality. Before turning to this, I would like to give some background on the evolution of my own Marian spirituality.

A Child Looks At Mary

AS A CATHOLIC CHILD in the fifties and early sixties I was typically devoted to Mary. In my family we recited the rosary, kneeling together in a circle. In the Catholic primary school I attended there were additional devotions: novenas, miraculous medals and the pageantry of the May crowning.

The crowning of Our Lady as queen of May typifies the Marian experience of my childhood. I associated Mary with Spring beauty, knit together in floral crown and placed on the head of the Madonna, standing in a niche of our Lourdes-replica stone grotto. I associated her with new life, and the first scent of roses in late Spring. She opened the season for miniature boxcar building, and I remember how we used our spare wood to build her little May altars. The novenas attended in nine May nights were sensual and whetted our appetite for the nocturnal neighborhood game of 'hide and seek' we played with devotion in the darkness among the budding maple trees. In childhood Mary was the door to summer, a sign that our holiday freedom was fast approaching.

I loved Mary when I was a little boy. I associated her with something primeval and immediate. She was my partner in exploration. She led me to the right rocks to turn over in my relentless pursuit of salamanders. She showed me the best place to sit for sighting pheasants, and stayed with me for hours until one appeared. She knew the source of Patterson creek, the name of each stellar constellation, and where to find arrowheads. She was a friend, a wise lady, a sojourner in the world of nature and discovery.

Mary, of course, was also my mother. This image of Mary corresponded very closely to the person of my own mother. She is a strong and compassionate woman presently in charge of emergency services for the poor at the Office of Catholic Charities in my hometown.

There are many people who have benefitted from my mother's strength and compassion. Two of us share the same benefit in common. She gave us back our ability to stand on our own two feet. I was born with clubfeet and would have had trouble standing if it were not for the leg braces I wore as an infant. My mother's determination gave me the courage to overcome this handicap. My brother was in a serious motorcycle accident. The doctors thought he would never stand again. Her challenging love stood him up and saved him from a life of immobility.

When she was a young girl my mother herself was unable to stand for an entire year. She had an illness that the family doctor said would leave her bedridden for life. But, characteristically, she did not believe him. With rock-strong determination she stood herself up. I sometimes wonder what would have happened to my brother and I decades later if that young girl had not been so determined.

The Stabat Mater, Mary standing at the foot of the cross, is one Marian posture of courage which will be explored in this book. It is translated as "Standing Mother."

An Adolescent Looks At Mary

WHEN I became an adolescent, Mary vanished from my life. I would hear about her now and then in lectures about modesty which we received periodically during religion class. But I grew to dislike her and didn't understand the purpose of saying a Hail Mary as a means of diverting my attention from the body I was beginning to discover. In my adolescent mind Mary became associated with rigidity and fear. I would describe our relationship in those years as frozen or temporarily on ice. This phase of the friendship continued well into my twenties, even after the stage of adolescent suspicion of the Church, and even after rediscovering the treasures of Catholicism.

A five month experience at the Catholic Worker House of Hospitality on First Street in the Lower East Side of New York City, when Dorothy Day was still alive, opened to me a deep meaning of the Gospel. I was on fire with personalism, with hospitality for homeless people in the Bowery, with anger at the waste of military spending and government disregard of the poor. I wanted to change the world and thought social action alone would do it. I joined the Peace

Corps in order to go to the Sahel of West Africa which, at the time, was slowly recovering from a seven-year famine. I needed to be in the thick of the action. Human suffering, I thought, was about to be overcome by sheer enthusiasm and pure idealism. I was wrong.

My Peace Corps post was an isolated village in the Republic of Niger in the West African Sahel. I was assigned to a high school to teach English.

I don't know how much English the students learned but my own mind was opened to a world of suffering for which I was totally unprepared. The number of hungry children, the vulnerability of people without adequate medicines and necessities for survival left me feeling overwhelmed and small.

My attempts to do something to improve the situation drew me up face to face with my own vulnerability. My failure in helping people and the fact that my attempts sometimes even hurt people made me question Christianity, or what I thought was Christianity. A new doubt was planted in my soul. And it could lead me in either of two directions. One direction, suggested to me by one I call the Master Deceiver, led to cynicism and the repudiation of human redemption. The other direction, suggested to me by the Spirit, led to a greater acceptance of myself through a deeper trust in Divine Providence.

An Adult Looks At Mary

WHEN I came back from West Africa I was hired by the University of Dayton to raise funds for a development project in the Sahel sponsored by the University. This job entailed close interaction with the Catholic religious congregation responsible for the University. Oddly enough, this congregation was called the Society of Mary.

I eventually joined this congregation, attracted by a certain quality in the men and women who were members. This was the beginning of my rediscovery of Mary. After my first three years as a professed Brother, while working with the poor in Nairobi, I began to recognize her as my mentor in courage. Until those three years in Nairobi, my Christianity was still an odd mixture of do-goodism and political idealism. Only gradually did I realize that few of my lofty goals would be achieved. I met this threatened disappointment at first with renewed effort, driving myself even harder. My understanding of the Gospel did not allow failure. How little I understood the Good News.

In spite of my stubborn refusal to recognize my limitations, and the limitations inherent in any development project, my body got through to me. I fell sick with an ulcer. The largest of the small business enterprises we had started for the poor went bankrupt. The world collapsed on my head. I became depressed and contemplated leaving the Brotherhood. I had obviously failed.

At this point in my life, stripped of the agenda and conditions I had claimed for my vocation, I began to understand the real meaning of vocation. The liturgical season was Advent. Mary was featured in many of the readings in the Divine Office and at Eucharist. We waited with her, sharing the longing and the emptiness she reserved for God. She symbolized all people who waited for God, who sometimes failed God but who never lost hope in God's promise. While I thought of her that Advent, I sensed my own emptiness being filled. The anger I felt at myself and at an unjust world began to be transformed into something more like courage. My failure and the failure of our projects for the poor, I realized, were materials God could still use to build the Kingdom.

I recognized then that each and every one was gifted with a unique vocation, a way in which he or she alone could fail. This happy weakness, the chipped gift we return to God through Christ, contains the chemical needed for the reaction-equation of redemption.

All this prepared me to face a second famine, the worst one in recent African history (1984/85). This time I approached the suffering in a new way. I did not feel guilty about it. I did not treat the famine as a personal affront or a trial of my self-worth. I was less preoccupied with proving myself.

I offered to God the hunger and our work at trying to relieve it. And when thoughts of failure or feelings of reproach appeared, I did not entertain them. These I also gave over to God.

While praying Mary's Magnificat with my brothers in community, a certain faith slowly deepened within me. I received a wonderful assurance that despite our faulty attempts at famine relief, the hungry would indeed be fed. I began to believe, in the words of Julian of Norwich, that "God makes all things well and all manner of things shall He make well."

Marian Faith

THIS BOOK is about faith. It is about Marian faith which exposes the seductive lie — a lie told to certain individuals and groups to make them feel unworthy and unable to change the inhuman conditions from which they suffer. It is about the faith of poor people and refugees for whom Mary is a spokesperson in the Magnificat. A faith that can nourish people.

This book is about the vision that faith engenders, a vision, disclosed in the Risen Christ, of a world made new. The words of Elizabeth describe well such a one with Kingdom eyes, "Happy (is she) to believe that the Lord's message . . . will come true" (Lk 1:48).

The faith of Mary can become our faith. Though she is sometimes depicted in paintings as swooning into the arms of St. John at the foot of the cross, in my experience she has played just the opposite role. Before every cross in my life, there stands Mary supporting me when I would swoon.

No matter how we find ourselves at the foot of the cross, it is a teachable moment, one in which we are disposed in a special way to receive the gift of faith. As the oriental expression puts it, "When the disciple is ready, a teacher appears." That is why Mary stands at the foot of the cross.

Mary cannot *give* us faith when we are at the foot of the cross for faith is a gift from God. She can, however, teach us the song of faith which, repeated often enough, like a child with his alphabet, will enable us to speak the language of God when faith is finally given to us.

In my vocabulary, faith and courage are in many ways synonymous. This is why I call Mary, the woman who stands at the foot of every cross, who teaches the Magnificat, singing it when faith is most tested, my mentor in courage.

The mission of Mary (and therefore the mission of the Church which she symbolizes) is to undo the despairing lie we believe about ourselves. The mission of Mary is to show the poor, the homeless, the rejected and all other oppressed people, through faith, their own special beauty and power in the place where they stand, at the foot of the cross. She is their mirror, their model, their image, their noble Icon.

2

THE
MASTER DECEIVER

Vocation and Temptation

I HAVE SAID the Lord's prayer for
many years, but I never understood the phrase, "lead
us not into temptation." Why, I questioned, would
God ever let his beloved be tempted: and, besides,
what sort of temptation does the Lord mean?

My solution to this quandary did not come from
Biblical research and I do not claim it as anything but
a personal solution. I see, however, a direct connection between the second petition in the Lord's prayer
"Thy Kingdom come," and the second to the last
petition "lead us not into temptation."

The connection I make between these two peti-
tions in the Lord's prayer arises out of a personal
temptation into which I am led by the circumstances

13

of my ministry, that temptation to doubt whether God's Kingdom shall *ever* come.

God calls me into circumstances where I am tempted to disbelieve the possibility of the Kingdom. God does not lead me into temptation. But there is a curious connection between temptation and the vocation to which God calls me.

At the crossroad of vocation and temptation, I meet the Master Deceiver. This is the tempter, the one who would seduce me to turn back because "I am not worthy" of the task, or would kill my vocation with the poisonous suggestion that "humanity is irredeemable."

It is important, therefore, to understand the Master Deceiver and so I attempt to describe here what I know of this trickster through my own experience of my vocation and that of other Christians.

Vocation's Foe

WHO IS the Master Deceiver? And how does he work?

The best way to understand how the Master Deceiver works is to study Revelation 12:1-9.

A great sign appeared in heaven.
A woman clothed with the sun . . . .
Because she was with child, she wailed
aloud in pain as she labored to give birth.

(Rv 12:1-2)

Then another sign appeared in the heaven:
it was a huge dragon . . . the ancient serpent . . .
the seducer of the whole world.   (Rv 12:3-9)

Then the dragon stood before the woman
about to give birth, ready to devour her child
when it should be born.   (Rv 12:4)

Note two signs appear. The first is a great sign. The second is another sign. The first is Mary, the expecting mother. The second is "the ancient serpent . . . the seducer of the whole world" (Rv 12:9).

Signs not only reveal but they can also conceal. In this text of Revelation we must choose between a revealing sign and a concealing sign, between the woman clothed with the sun wailing aloud in pain to give birth to the Light and the ancient serpent who would devour that Light to seduce the whole world.

The ancient serpent is intent on deception. It tricked the mother and father of humankind by making them despise their humanity and strive for what they were not. It tried to devour the Light to which Mary gave birth because in that Light we know our true worth. The Master Deceiver uses every opportunity to wield his weapons of distortion, making us despise ourselves so we end up in despair.

The Master Deceiver is that power of evil in our lives which urges us to hate ourselves and even to destroy ourselves. The seducing sign.

The Master Deceiver tells the dispossessed that they deserve their poverty, that they are loathsome failures. The Master Deceiver tells the refugees that they deserve their exile, that they are unacceptable rejects.

Why this deception? Quite simply there exists no other weapon against the good except to distort it.

Evil is actually a weakling who must resort to cheap tricks. What we hate about ourselves, what we fear, what persistently tries to intimidate and manipulate us, that awful vision of ourselves as a failure and a reject, is nothing else but a trick done with mirrors.

Many vocations lose their bearings and founder in the distorting light of these dreadful mirrors. "How did I ever imagine I could do that with my life? After all, I am uneducated, I don't come from the right background, I am not the right race or sex."

This may have been a ploy used by the Master Deceiver against Mary. She may very well have been tempted to stop her ears at the Annunciation, or reply in the negative rather than utter her "Fiat," or hide herself in shame rather than proclaim the Gospel to her cousin Elizabeth.

The Master Deceiver may have tried to dupe her into rejecting her vocation on the grounds that she wasn't educated enough, or wealthy enough, that she wasn't from the right tribe of Israel, or from the right place, that she was, in short, no good, a failure and a reject.

But Mary believed the promise made by God to a dispossessed people. She believed in the hospitality of God to an exiled people. And she accepted his invitation for her to become the mother of the Messiah.

The Master Deceiver could not sink this vocation. Mary heard God's call, responded "yes," and proclaimed to Elizabeth, and to all of us, the fidelity and generosity of God: "He has lifted up the lowly . . . filled the hungry with good things (and) . . . helped Israel his servant . . . (as) he promised" (Lk 1:52-55).

Principalities And Powers

THE MASTER DECEIVER works through what St. Paul calls the principalities and powers, that is, through the fallen world and its fallen creatures. Institutions, even well-meaning institutions, often typify the behavior of fallen creatures.

Along with the true we learn some untrue things about ourselves through certain institutions. A great many of these (many times unintentionally) give us a distorted, unhealthy image of ourselves. A typical example is the grading system of primary schools and the focus on pass, fail. Another is a national economic system where self-worth is measured by salary grade. Or still another example is an international economic system that writes off certain developing countries as "basket cases," unworthy of the global "lifeboat." Much could also be said of institutional patriarchy with its vocabulary about women that detracts from their humanity.

In one way or another the Master Deceiver uses the principalities and powers to convince us that we are "no good," that we have failed and we are unloved. The Master Deceiver proclaims "Bad News."

I have seen the Master Deceiver at work in the lives of the poor. During the 1984/85 African famine (caused not only by drought but by a principality called the International Economic System) some of these poor people said that they deserved it, that they were being punished for being "bad people." And again when certain development projects failed some of the poor were heard to say, "We told you so"; others recited a litany of "can'ts" ascribed to their own bad habits, routine, "the way things are" or "who *we* are". The Master Deceiver has such people precisely where he wants them.

A good example of the tactics of the Master Deceiver was given by Jesus in the "Parable of the Prodigal Son." This younger son left home, took his father's money and had a good time in a foreign country. When the money was gone he chose to eat with the pigs, lamenting his unworthiness. Through the victim's self-hatred the Master Deceiver had the boy just where he likes to keep us all. The prodigal son believed he was no good, a rat of a son, a failure. The Master Deceiver is delighted when this "Bad News" defines the way things are and who we think we are.

In my own life I have found myself in this pig sty of self-loathing. On returning to the USA from Niger I seriously considered never going back to Africa because I felt that I had failed the hungry people in my village. I voiced my own litany of "can'ts" to my spiritual director: weak stomach, scruples, over-sensitivity, etc. The Master Deceiver was feeding me swill not fit for human consumption.

Mary's Vocation

IN SPIRITUAL DIRECTION I was given Mary as a model of fidelity to one's vocation. The outset of her calling, after all, was not exactly a series of successes. And certainly there were doubts that assailed her.

The "Hail Mary" can be considered a pious prayer made up of a lot of holy sentiments. But to the one who first heard them from the lips of an Angel, it was a greeting filled with frightening words.

Blessed are you among women and
blessed is the fruit of your womb, Jesus.

The "Good News" singled out this young woman for a unique vocation in the history of the world.

It set Mary apart: not in a triumphalistic way, but, rather, in a way which was no less alienating. She suddenly became an unwed mother. She was cast outside the confines of the socially acceptable. She was a mother without a husband, and an affront to her culture.

The good news marginalized Mary. The fruit of her womb, the two-edged sword, cut the umbilical cord that bound Mary to popular expectations, and set her among the outcast. Now she, too, was an exile. She, too, was a Samaritan. She, too, was a leper and a cripple. She, too, was a marginal person along with the publicans and prostitutes.

When Mary was evangelized, she was also marginalized. The sign of this evangelization, her swelling belly, was also the cause of her marginalization. Her "yes" marked her in a more scandalous way than any scarlet letter.

What doubts assailed Mary during her time in Bethlehem? While still pregnant she was ascribed a number by the reigning principality. To Rome she was a nameless subject, a nobody save for the scribble of the census taker. She was deprived of a name by the oppressor which would just as soon that she forget her identity altogether. Mary's temptation in this imperial census is to think of herself as a non-person.

The Master Deceiver used many such ploys to make Mary reject herself and her vocation: pregnancy out of wedlock, the distress of her husband, the inhospitality of the innkeeper, the chill of the stable, and the unanswered questioning in her own heart.

What doubts affected Mary during the flight into Egypt, after the slaughter of the innocents? Maybe she was tempted to think her vocation was bogus. Look at the fruit: so many children massacred, their mothers wailing, inconsolable. Maybe she had made a mistake? Maybe she was not the one through whom the Messiah would come? Who was she after all? Or maybe, worse yet, humanity was irredeemable. Look how much evil had been unleashed. Behold the power of the principalities. What could a refugee family do against it?

3

THE SEDUCTION OF POVERTY

The Lie

MY RELIGIOUS COMMUNITY is involved in a program to assist squatters in the city of Nairobi, the capital of Kenya.

The squatters' village is close to our house. It consists of many igloo-shaped shacks made of polyethylene plastic, sticks and pieces of cardboard piled on top of semi-spherical bamboo frames. The occupants of these 12' x 9' x 6' houses are mostly women and children.

Their main source of income is derived from collecting old bones from butchers and selling them to fertilizer companies. They also collect tin cans for recycling. It seems there is never enough money for food, clothing and medicine. The children, in particular, suffer from the lack of these necessities.

21

The squatters are often made to feel that they deserve their plight. *Shauri ya Mungu* they call it — *the will of God*. But, in fact, it is the will of the principalities and powers. The message is that the squatters deserve their plight because they are simply unable . . . they can't do anything to help themselves.

On occasion I have met a certain kind of squatter who makes me feel very uncomfortable. This is the poor person who has accepted the lie inherent in all oppression. This is the person who believes, "I am nobody, no good, not worthy, not capable." In such a person the oppressive force has claimed a victory.

There is one such individual who used to come to our house to beg. Now there is nothing wrong in begging. Sometimes to be a beggar requires a lot of self-respect. But this poor soul had none. He would begin by saying, "I can't *help* myself." Then he would recite a litany of all the things which incapacitated him: he had a bad leg, he was illiterate, his children were ingrates, he had no one to take care of him. And, as always, would I help? Indeed, this man believed the lie.

This beggar reminded me of the cripple lying at the edge of the pool of Bethesda who stayed there thirty-eight years because, as he explained, "There is no one to help me to the water" (Jn 5:7). He, too, was a captive of the lie.

It is beyond any stretch of the imagination that no one in thirty-eight years offered to help the cripple of Bethesda. He was simply a victim of the insidious "I can't" ruse. And Jesus commanded him to take up his mat and walk. Note that Jesus didn't pity him, even though the cripple wanted pity. Instead, Jesus drove out the demon of self-deprecation. He challenged the man to stand up!

One day as my visitor went on about his incapacities and lowered himself ever deeper into a mire of self-pity, I wanted to shout, "Jesus Christ has risen for you! Stop doing this to yourself! Please! You are worth infinity and nothing is in your way but an ugly, insipid lie!" I wanted to challenge him to stand up. Instead I gave him another handout.

That day I realized how little I knew about sharing my faith. I wish I had had the courage to show that beggar his dignity, power and beauty. I wish I had known how to smash the false image which so victimized him. But I, too, had been seduced by poverty.

The experience made it clear to me that I needed a mentor, someone who saw through the lie, someone who could deepen my faith in God's power to "lift up the lowly" (Lk 1:52).

The Dispossessed Of Israel

MARY DID NOT ACCEPT the terms of the oppressor. She never once thought of herself as a failure. She did not mistrust herself. Her faith was undisturbed by the manipulations of those in power. She could not be forced to feel inferior or incapable or third class. She did not accept the terms of the oppressor. She defined herself.

Mary was able to define herself because she was not dispossessed of the past. She knew the story of her people. She claimed her inheritance. And for this reason she was not dispossessed of the future.

Indeed, Mary refused to accept a future determined by oppressive forces. To her, the future was defined by God's promise. She was empowered by this promise, a promise which God had made to Israel.

Poverty, according to Albert Gelin, shocked the ancient Israelites. It was scandalous! When Moses led the people of God into the desert, they were formed into a living body and shared their possessions as they shared a common experience of liberation from slavery. The disparities between rich and poor which developed over the years as the people settled in the land of Canaan puzzled and perturbed those who reflected on their original vision of the "promised land."

The prophets cried out against this state of affairs. They even traced its origin. They pointed to two major causes: large landholding by the nobility and the extravagant luxuries of the king.

Larger landholdings became the primary goal for many: the lust for increased acreage, disregarding the terms of the tenth commandment as formulated by Moses (Ex 20:17).

> Seizing the fields that they covet,
> they take over the houses as well.
> Owner and house they confiscate together,
> taking both men and inheritance.   (Mi 2:2)

The prophets could not understand how this "promised land" could be more promised for some and less promised for others. The luxuries of the king impoverished the poor. Far worse, they blinded the king to justice.

> Like a cage full of birds,
> so are their houses full of loot;
> because of it, they grow fat and sleek.
> Yes, in wickedness they go to any lengths.
> They have no respect for justice,
> or for orphans' rights, to support them;
> they do not uphold the cause of the poor.
>
> (Jr 5:27-28)

The kings, according to the prophets, were not like Moses. Binding themselves to their own wealth, they were unable to recognize how they bound their own people.

The prophetic literature describes how the people of God, once a single body, broke into different groupings. First there was the king, then the nobility, and finally the others. This last group had several different names: *ebyon, dal* and *ani*.

The *ebyon* is the poor person who is always seeking and begging. The word implies both a need as well as an expectation or a request. Gelin suggests that the word might be a foreign expression introduced into Hebrew when persons, who had property taken from them, began to beg.

The *dal* is the poor person who is physically impoverished. He is emaciated, weak and visibly ill. This word appears in the stereotyped expression *dallat ha'ares*, the "thin one of the land," which Gelin points out is another way of indicating the rural proletariat.

The *ani* is the poor person whose power and worth have declined as a result of "suffering due to economic poverty, sickness, prison, or oppression." The root of this word originally meant "to be stooped, bowed, lowered, overwhelmed."* The *ani* is the person who had been made low.

All three words express a kind of changed status. People who had been participants in Israel's liberation from bondage find the tables turned on them. In a strange twist, the just are hated and the wealthy are without integrity:

> Those who turn justice into wormwood
> throwing integrity to the ground;
> who hate the man dispensing justice at the city
> gate and detest those who speak with honesty.
> (Am 5:7)

One word that might bring together the nuances of these three words is "*the dispossessed.*" This expression catches the descriptive boldness of all three Hebrew words. There were not simply the king, the nobility and the poor. No, this last group was not simply poor. They were "dispossessed." They had a history. There were political reasons for their present status. The prophets refused to use a vocabulary of caste distinctions. They recognized the fallacy of simply calling these people poor. Hebrew does not allow for a description of the "poor" which would obscure the historical circumstances which created the *ebyon*, the *dal* and the *ani* out of the single people of God.

* Albert Gelin, *The Poor of Yahweh*, Collegeville, MN: Liturgical Press, 1964.

The dispossessed of Israel never thought they deserved their status. Their religious heritage did not legitimize the structure of oppression. They had been trapped. They had crossed the Red Sea as a single body. Together they had wandered in the desert, and together they had received the promise.

Every Israelite was a liberated Israelite. Each had received a promise. Even though dispossessed, they clung to the promise. They, therefore, never thought of themselves as permanently dispossessed. They never accepted their poverty or another's poverty as part of God's plan. And indeed, it most certainly was not.

The memory of liberation and the trust in the promise gave these people a certain self-image. The way they thought of themselves protected them from succumbing to any status of inferiority forced on them.

This image survived the passing centuries. It survived and etched itself ever deeper in the hearts of the dispossessed — so deep that it became a dream, and a prayer.

> May Yahweh be a stronghold for the oppressed,
> a stronghold when times are hard.
> Those who acknowledge your name
> can rely on you.
> Never desert those who seek you, Yahweh. . . .
> For the needy are not always forgotten;
> the hope of the poor is never brought to nothing.
> (Ps 9:10-11, 19)

The Dispossessed Woman

BIBLE SCHOLARS SAY that in the Magnificat St. Luke designated Mary as the spokesperson for the dispossessed of Israel.

In her beautiful hymn of praise, Mary recognizes herself to be an *ebyon,* a beggar. In this, she shares the consciousness of the urban destitute.

In the Magnificat, Mary sees herself as a *dal,* a thin one of the land. In this, she shares the consciousness of the rural proletariat.

In the Magnificat, Mary proclaims herself to be one of the *ani,* the oppressed. In this, she shares the consciousness of those made low by social structures of injustice.

The Magnificat image Mary had of herself as *dal, ebyon* and *ani* shaped her response to the oppressive forces in the world. She was not submissive.

The fact of dispossession is radically different from the consciousness of submission. Mary claimed her heritage as one of the participants in Israel's liberation from slavery. Her posture would have been, "I was made for something better than this." And she protested.

The oppressor told her that she belonged to a conquered people in a remote part of a remote colony. The oppressor looked at her as an unmarried, pregnant teenager who had made a mistake. The oppressor might have suggested an abortion, a practice rampant in the Roman Empire.

"Fiat": May It Be Done To Me According To Your Word (Lk 1:38).

WHAT CAN BE SAID about Mary's "Fiat"? We could say she said "yes" to becoming the mother of a new humanity. She welcomed the Kingdom within her.

What a terrible unknown she welcomed. These days the word, "Kingdom," has become overused. When any word is overused, people tend to think they've captured it, and know what it means. Mary opened herself to something as wild as the sea and as unknown as the spray of Milky Way stars. In her womb, the anxious universe, storm-swept by powers of darkness, became re-created. Into her womb the fury of every human tempest rushed, as if she were a wind tunnel, and this became the hurricane of Redemption. To everything human she said "yes," making everything human a vessel for God's revolution.

It is by her "Fiat" that Mary performs her greatest act of defiance:

> To let God's mercy reach from age to age,
> she said, "yes."
> To let God show the power of His arm,
> she said "yes."
> To let God destroy the proud of heart,
> she said "yes."
> To let God pull down princes from their thrones,
> she said "yes."

> To let God exalt the lowly,
>   she said "yes."
> To let God fill the hungry with good things,
>   she said "yes."
> To let God enlighten the rich concerning their
>   emptiness, she said "yes."
> To let God come down to the help of his people,
>   she said "yes."

"Yes" is a *mighty* little word. Those who use it create a beachhead, a forward point in the battle of Redemption. By saying "yes" to a different reality they use the "as if" key. They live "as if" they were beloved. And they love. They live "as if" the world can become just. And there is justice. They live "as if" the Kingdom has come. And it arrives. These people are seen as fools. Yet they, of all people, are the ones who are wise.

The "Fiat" shows the power of poetry. Mary disregards what others keep insisting is fact. And, by using the "as if" key, she opens the Messianic age. She disregards hate, ugliness, and injustice; living "as if" the Magnificat were already fact.

In spite of the clever ruses of the Master Deceiver, Mary was not seduced into cynicism. Fidelity to her own dignity (faith in herself) and to God's promise helped her withstand the seduction of poverty.

Indeed, she was made for something better, for that better world which her "Fiat" could usher in. While one kind of pride (a selfish kind of hubris) brought about the Fall, the wholesome pride of this impoverished, pregnant teenager brought about the Redemption.

4

THE SEDUCTION OF EXILE

The Homeless

IN AFRICA today there are 2.5 million refugees. In fact, one in every 200 Africans is a refugee. The African continent has more than a quarter of the world's ten million refugees, although it has less than a tenth of the world's population.

Several brothers in my community work with refugees in Nairobi. These refugees come from Uganda, Ethiopia, South Africa, Zaire and other African countries.

The reasons they come to Nairobi are varied. Some are political refugees. They are fleeing to save themselves from persecution. Some are economic refugees. They are fleeing famine in the rural areas, or unemployment in the urban areas of their countries. In every case, refugees leave an intolerable situation hoping to find a new and better life in a strange and often distant land.

People far away from home are especially vulnerable to the seduction of the Master Deceiver. All the usual props and supports are gone. Outside one's culture, distant from family and friends, one is tempted by a value vacuum. Questions arise. "Who am I?" "What am I worth?" "What is anything worth?"

In the Peace Corps we used to say that such an experience would make or break a person. And it was true. Some volunteers discovered themselves, recognized greater inner resources of fortitude and compassion. Others declined — morally and spiritually. They treated Africans in ways they would never have treated people back home. The magnitude of suffering around them crippled their faith so much that first year volunteers were shocked by the indifference and cynicism they heard in the conversation of these second year volunteers.

Of course, this is not only true of Peace Corps volunteers. It happens to missionaries, development specialists and every sort of expatriate. One of the best illustrators of this phenomenon is Graham Greene, especially in his book, *A Burnt-Out Case*. Joseph Conrad in his work, *Heart of Darkness*, also describes what happens to a person outside his own culture, lost in the value vacuum.

What happens in these cases of cynical volunteers, missionaries and other expatriates is the same thing that happens to many refugees. It is what I call the seduction of exile. One questions everything (which sometimes might be helpful), but then ends up believing in nothing.

Outside one's own culture one has a unique opportunity to realize new values. But many prefer instead to rub the sore of loss, remorse and loneliness. The only real world is that home far away, that inaccessible place beyond the blue horizon. And so one stoically enters the limbo of "nowhere" rather than make a new home "somewhere." One chooses to be alone and finds satisfaction in withdrawal.

A deceiving inner voice says, "I would be happier remembering how I once lived and how I once loved rather than to risk living and loving again." Nostalgia, then, substitutes for passion; fantasy, for real life. Nostalgia becomes a subtle form of cynicism.

The alternative to this seduction is a leap of faith . . . to trust another culture, to trust another people. In this way one escapes the value vacuum that creates cynicism. And slowly one integrates these new values with other values, and answers in a new way the questions of "Who am I?" "What am I worth?" "What is the value of anything?"

The ability to receive others different from ourselves, even challenging others to recognize their own worth, is what I call hospitality. And here, again, Mary is our mentor.

The Refugees of Israel

As a refugee, Mary is not duped by the Master Deceiver into a cynicism of remorse or nostalgia. It is true that she had lost her home in her family's flight to Egypt. But her people had a story of exile and return that nourished her. She knew that the experience of exile was also a call to pilgrimage, a summons by the Divine Host to a deeper appreciation of the value of hospitality.

In 587 B.C. Judea fell to the Babylonians. The elite were carried off into captivity. They became exiles far from the familiar security of the "promised land."

This "seventy year period" of exile did not destroy Israel's faith. On the contrary, it strengthened it. All the props were gone. God could not be found in a building or in divine privileges or in an elite or in any man-made structure. When the people lost their land, God again was found.

It was during the Babylonian exile that God truly formed a people of passionate longing; Israel discovered its heart.

> I shall give you a new heart and put a new spirit within you; I shall remove the heart of stone from your bodies and give you a heart of flesh instead. You will live in the land I gave your ancestors. You shall be my people and I shall be your God.   (Ezk 36:26-28)

The prophets during the exile gave hope to a dejected people who were lost in the value vacuum of Babylon. In the writings of these prophets one sees the image of God and the image of home interface. Longing for God and longing for Jerusalem became nearly equivalent.

May I never speak again
if I forget you!
If I do not count Jerusalem
the greatest of my joys.   (Ps 137:6)

The longing to go home became a powerful religious experience that went beyond travelling back to Palestine. Jerusalem became a symbol for God's Kingdom, a place of justice and peace. And the Jewish people became pilgrims on their way to this better world.

To her image of God as Liberator (Ex 14), and to her image of God as the Just One (Mi 2:2, Jr 5:27, Am 5:7), Israel now added a new image: that of God who summons his people home to a new Zion. In second Isaiah especially, we encounter the Divine Host:

Oh, come to the water all you who are thirsty;
though you have no money come!
Buy corn without money and eat,
and at no cost, wine and milk.   (Is 55:1)

God played host to a refugee people in such a way that they came to a new understanding of their exile. They were more than refugees, they were sojourners and pilgrims.

The Refugee Mother

JESUS OF NAZARETH was a man of hospitality. It seems odd to describe him this way since he had no place to lay his head. How could a vagabond excel in this virtue? How could a homeless man have ever said, "Come to me all you who are weary and I will refresh you." Yet despite his apparent lack of domestic resources, the characteristic mark of the mobile ministry of Jesus was his welcome to strangers and sinners, the sick and the rejected who needed to feel at home.

Jesus learned hospitality from the one who first offered it to him in her womb. He made the leap from one world to a new one. And he made that leap through Mary.

As a refugee Mary had learned a lot about hospitality. She knew how to receive people in such a way that they could receive themselves. She knew about culture-shock and the way one could get through it. Could it be said that Mary helped Jesus make the transition from one culture to a new and alien one? Or can one properly speak of a heavenly culture and an earthly one? In any case, this refugee mother was the first to host Jesus.

Here is a mother who did not protect her child from strangers. She, rather, presented him to gentile visitors from the East.

In Western art these visitors are depicted as wise men and kings. The Gospel writer's intent, suggest some Bible scholars, is not to portray respectable kings but, rather, to show that even Magi, sorcerers, wicked gentile magicians, sinners, rejects of society are welcome by the Infant Lord. In fact, his holy family consists of just such people. We are that family.

In the Nazareth home of the refugee mother, Jesus learns to welcome strangers, sinners and those who are rejected.

Pilgrim Host

IN THE GOSPELS Mary is often depicted leaving home to go to some new place. She leaves Nazareth to go to visit Elizabeth in Judea. She leaves Nazareth for Bethlehem to be counted in the Imperial census. She leaves Nazareth to find safety in Egyptian exile. She leaves Nazareth to go to the temple in Jerusalem. She leaves Nazareth to attend a wedding in Cana. The Gospel shows her as a woman on the move, a pilgrim woman.

In all her journeys Mary has a destination and a purpose. She pilgrims forth in order to play hostess.

Though forced to leave Nazareth by Imperial decree she makes a comfortable dwelling of a dirty stable, the first home of the holy family. Then, with the slaughter of the innocents and government threats against her child, she and her family flee from their old community and make a new home in an unfamiliar land.

The purpose of Mary's journeys is well illustrated in John's description of the wedding feast at Cana. When the wine jugs were empty, Mary filled the vacuum by challenging the servants, who feared the void, to believe in "whatever He tells you." She helped them overcome their cynicism, for they did not hesitate to carry the contents of the water jugs to the head steward to taste. In this journey Mary had created a milieu in which new wine and new faith filled an embarrassing emptiness. This special guest had really played hostess for that Kingdom which Cana foreshadowed (Jr 2:1-11).

In the next two journeys of the Pilgrim Hostess which we shall examine, Mary provides the background for people asking the questions: "Who am I? What am I worth? What is the value of anything?" Both stories in the Gospel of Luke (2:41-52; 1:39-56) show persons becoming aware of their authentic self in her presence.

Jesus is portrayed journeying with Mary, as they return from their pilgrimage to the temple. He then speaks for the first time in Luke's Gospel. These words indicate his self-awareness: "I must be about my Father's business." In this Gospel story the lost child is found or, rather discovers himself . . . a premonition is given him of his pilgrim life on earth.

Elizabeth is visited by Mary. In Mary's presence Elizabeth grasps the significance of the curious events of the preceding months and recognizes her vocation. It kicks within her. And then we are given the words which explain all of Mary's journeys, the message she spreads whether in silence or in song:

> He has stretched out his mighty arm
> and scattered the proud with all their plans.
> He has brought down mighty kings from their thrones and has lifted up the lowly.
> He has filled the hungry with good things
> and sent the rich away with empty hands. . . .
> He has kept the promise . . .   (Lk 1:51-55)

It was away from home, while on a pilgrimage of hospitality, that Mary spoke these words to an old woman, dispelling any cynicism that age and sterility may have produced in Elizabeth. Emptiness is filled, indeed, with good things.

Each time this Pilgrim Hostess reaches her destination things begin to happen. Through her mobile hospitality at Elizabeth's house, at Bethlehem's stable, in hiding and at the wedding feast at Cana, Mary confronts the seduction of exile. She challenges those who are in the Void, who are tempted by homelessness and rootlessness.

The challenge is simple. What one experiences in exile may, in fact, be a call to pilgrimage and an opportunity to render hospitality to sojourners.

5

MARY,
MENTOR IN COURAGE

Hibernation
Or Proclamation

IN OUR TROUBLED WORLD, there
are two possible lives for one to choose: hibernation
or Gospel proclamation. Choosing the first is safe for
the individual but risky for the world. Choosing the
second is risky for the individual but shall save the
world including, paradoxically, everything one may
have risked.

To proclaim the Gospel requires courage. In my
journey as a Marianist I have discovered that the best
mentor for such courage is Mary, the first to risk
herself for the Gospel. The following two stories tell
of two different African famines in which I discovered Mary as a mentor in courage, a virtue that in
my vocabulary is now synonymous with faith, a gift
that is offered to all.

41

Mariama

WHEN I WENT as a Peace Corps volunteer to Niger in 1975 the Sahelian drought had just ended. The famine killed 100,000 people.

The effect of the catastrophe lingered. In the remote village where I was teaching English, visitors came to my door every evening asking for food. Trying to respond to their need, I soon discovered my own limitations.

I struggled with faith. How could God *allow* such suffering? Where was God in the midst of such need? I disputed with the local Marabout (an Islamic teacher). As a devout Moslem, he prayed seven times a day. I bluntly told him that if God existed he was most certainly not listening.

On Christmas night in 1975, feeling sorry for myself so far away from home, I heard a knock on the door. When I opened it, I saw a woman standing there holding a child about a year old. The child was suffering from marasmus, a disease of malnutrition.

The mother asked me for some milk. I managed to get a liter of goat's milk and gave it to her. As she disappeared into the dark, I thought that that was the last I would ever see of her. The next day, however, she was back.

She continued coming to my house for two weeks. During this time I learned that her name was Mariama, or Mary. Day after day she went away with that liter of goat's milk. At the end of the second week, I was holding the child and noticed that he had gained weight. It occurred to me that I had never even asked the child's name. And so I asked. She told me that the child's name was Issa.

You can imagine my stupefaction! "Issa," you see, is translated "Jesus." On Christmas night a woman named Mary had come to my house with a child named Jesus. And she had even asked for my hospitality.

After she left, I went to my room in a fog. I fell to my knees. And, for the first time in many weeks, I started to pray.

Following an urging, I got up and went out into the streets of the village. Walking along I saw something new in the faces of those hungry people. In each one I recognized the face of Issa, the face of Christ, the whereabouts of God. Without the Marabout telling me, I discovered where God was. Indeed, I knew in a way that I had never known before, that God *is* truly with us. He is our Emmanuel.

The suffering continued. Malnourished people kept coming to my house. And still I questioned why God allowed such suffering. Eventually I stopped disputing with the local Marabout. Instead I argued with God.

And what began as a quarrel, soon became a long and drawn out conversation.

Courage That Sings

DURING THE TEN YEARS between the Sahelian famine and the East African famine, I joined the Marianists. I persisted in my questioning about human suffering. It is still a mystery to me. I suspect it shall remain so as long as I live. I have now, though — thanks to the Marianists — made acquaintance with a mentor who enables me to live with joy and with mystery at the same time.

This mentor appeared during the recent African famine. Countless people throughout the continent were on the brink of starvation. Twenty-seven of the 50 African nations had declared themselves in a state of famine. With over half of Kenya affected, we gathered together each evening to sing the Magnificat. How I struggled to believe the words that my lips uttered!

How could I believe Mary's words about the hungry being fed and the lowly raised up? Didn't all the evidence prove just the contrary? Hopelessness was an easy friend.

But as I sang the Magnificat in the face of famine, the terms of faith became clearer. We must *choose* whether or not to believe that the world can be different. Faith demands our commitment to a promised world.

Mary's commitment to that world initiated its fulfillment in Jesus Christ. Thus her faith is a prototype of all faith. She was aware of the hard evidence of a suffering world and understood its challenge to faith. Nonetheless, she risked being foolish enough to believe God's promise. And she gave that promise birth.

I asked myself then if I were foolish enough. I was reminded of the play, "Man of La Mancha." Charging windmills as if they were giants, and stabbing the thin air with his sword, Don Quixote behaved as a fool. Not a single demon did he destroy, except for the one of hopelessness which lived in the breast of El Donza, the whore.

She started to believe his silly vision of a world made right. With him she began to sing of the impossible dream. And she became Dulcinea, the visionary. Singing the Magnificat with my brothers during the famine made me realize my likeness to El Donza. The demon of hopelessness jumped about in my breast, too, like a toad on hot tar. The words of the Magnificat were a lump in my throat. I swallowed hard, as one on the edge of an abyss. But the more I said that "the hungry will be fed with good things," the more I wanted to believe it. And I began to ask God for the gift of faith.

The months passed. The famine continued. As I became involved with the food relief efforts of the Kenya Catholic Secretariat, I met lay people, sisters, brothers and priests, who were seeing terrible human misery. Yet, even though faced with such suffering, they were not anxious. They went about the work of famine relief with a peace of mind that startled me.

Gradually, as I sang the Magnificat in the evening with my brothers, I experienced a growing consolation. And during the day, while doing famine relief work, I, too, became less and less anxious. Something inside me was giving way. I was letting go. Perhaps I was stepping down from my self-appointed position as manager of the universe and letting God be God.

And as I was letting go, I was also receiving. I was given the faith to believe the promise of the Magnificat; I had opened myself in a deeper way to Jesus, the Lord, the one who fulfills that promise.

I had, at last, become foolish enough. The crazy expectation voiced first by Mary became my song; and Christ became my source of courage.

For we were so utterly and unbearably crushed that we despaired of life. . . . But that was to make us rely not on ourselves but on God who raises from the dead; He delivered us . . . and He will deliver us; on Him we have set our hope that He will deliver us again.   (2 Cor 1:8-10)

Temptation And Vocation

THE FUNDAMENTAL CHOICE before every human being is whether to hope or not to hope, whether to accept the empowering promise of God or to fall for the big lie. The question of becoming a believer, then, has nothing to do with this or that difficult dogma or ecclesial scandal. The decision to become a Christian revolves on whether one chooses to accept the incredible Good News about reality disclosed in Jesus Christ: that reality is ultimately gracious, not malign; that life's troubles, in fact, are packed with grace.

Those very circumstances which first lead us into the temptation of cynicism, if offered to God, become conduits of grace and call. They are far from stumbling blocks; they are, in truth, helpful stepping stones.

6

SINGING THE PROMISE OF THE POOR

"He has lifted up the lowly."
(Lk 1:52)

A Bereaved Mother

ONE DAY in November of 1983 I was driving in the funeral cortege of a twelve year old girl from squatters' town. I used our van to carry the corpse to the cemetery. After the burial, the mother sat down beside me for the trip back home. An instant before I started the engine, I looked over at her.

She was sitting tall with her back straight. Her head was tilted back, she was looking up. She pushed out her chin like someone about to step from a warm house into bitter cold. She pressed her lips tight against each other like a runner in the last few meters

47

of a race. She was staring hard at the horizon above some distant hills, as if trying to make out something in the gathering darkness.

There was an expression of icy courage in those dry resolute eyes. The posture and tension of her body set her against some awful force. She was, I think, contending with that terrible temptation to consider her life futile. It appeared that her whole being was crying out "NO!" against this desperate lie.

At home, later that evening, I thought of Michelangelo's Pietà. The setting is a sad one. Mary is dispossessed of what she valued most. The great dreamer holds in her arms a crushed dream. She has lost not only a loved one but a promised world.

The face of Michelangelo's Mary, however, is serene. She closes her eyes, looking within. There is strength in the right arm which holds her crucified son. There is courage in the other arm which extends an open hand of prayer, accepting God's will. She is sitting tall with her back straight. The posture and tension of her body are poised against the lie of futility.

When I realized how these two women mirrored each other, I began to think how infrequently oppressed people get a true picture of themselves. Rather, they are given many unflattering reflections. They are made to see themselves as unable, unworthy, unlikely to succeed. These various negative images can form the consciousness of the oppressed and might yield people unlikely to smash the diabolical distorting mirror which robs them of their real identity.

The squatters need a different image of themselves if they are to believe that they are able, worthy, and likely to succeed. St. Paul describes well the kind of image which poor people need.

> And with our unveiled faces reflecting like mirrors the brightness of the Lord, all grow brighter and brighter as we are turned into the image we reflect: This is the work of the Lord who is Spirit. (2 Cor 3:18)

I thank God for that brief moment when I looked over at this bereaved mother and caught a glimpse of one such face unveiled, mirroring that promise which empowers the dispossessed.

A Good Friday Dance

EVERY GOOD FRIDAY the people in the squatters' village carry around their neighborhood a life-size cross made of two old, rough pieces of wood. One year I participated in this procession.

While I walked alongside the growing crowd, I tried to entertain what I thought were proper reflections for Good Friday. I thought of the hungry kids in squatters' town. I thought of the plastic and/or cardboard houses which were ever collapsing. I thought of how these people were like the crucified one. It was all very pious and somber. But as the procession continued I started to realize that others were not sharing these reflections. People were singing happy songs. Their step was light and buoyant. The procession received cheers from bystanders. The cross was lifted very high above the heads of all. It seemed to float atop the swelling throng. Some of the women were even dancing. The scene was joyous, triumphant!

The squatters were looking at the cross in a different way than I was. They were not pitying Jesus or getting sympathetic feelings about the misery of the world. Instead they were seeing the crucified Jesus as someone who not only suffered, but managed to take this suffering and turn it into victory. Jesus didn't just die and get snuffed out; a story they all know too well. Rather, he turned hunger, poor housing and destitution into something more. He gave meaning and promise to the very cross which they carry throughout the year, which truly has the cruel capacity to crush them. The death and Resurrection of Jesus made that same cross a window of final triumph. The cross which this Good Friday crowd lifted so high, was the winning trump card God played on their behalf. Why pity themselves? Why be afraid? The game had already been won!

On the cross, in what appears as defeat, God has won the decisive victory over sin, death and every oppression. Good Friday is a day for dancing.

The Conquerors

BAHATI IS another low-income neighborhood where we work. The word means "good-luck," which the residents feel is theirs since they live in stone houses. During the period of the Mau Mau (1950s), when Kenyans were fighting for their independence, Bahati was a colonial detention camp for any Kikuyu person in Nairobi without proper identification.

The people *are* "lucky" to live in stone houses. But other conditions in Bahati are not all that fortunate. There is much overcrowding. Cubes originally built for single men now are occupied by whole families. The most unfortunate condition in Bahati, and throughout the city of Nairobi, is a very high rate of unemployment. This leads to drug and alcohol abuse, crime, and a sense of hopelessness.

A group of young people in Bahati discussed their problems and made a commitment to each other to complete their parents' struggle for freedom by becoming economically self-reliant. In this spirit they started a small business cooperative. They now make batik pictures of various animals and are developing a larger market so that more unemployed young people can be given a job. They call themselves *Ushindi* which means "conquerors." And whenever they greet each other at work they say *"Tutashinda"* which means, "We will win." The origin of this name comes from the following text in St. Paul's letter to the Romans which is often read at prayer meetings in the poor neighborhoods of East Nairobi.

Who shall separate us from the love of Christ? Shall tribulation, or distress, or persecution, or famine, or nakedness, or peril, or sword? . . . No. In all these things we are more than conquerors through him who loved us. For I am certain

that nothing can separate us from this love:
neither death nor life . . . neither principalities
and powers. . . ." (Rm 8:35, 37, 38)

Jesus says that the meek shall inherit the earth
(Mt 5:5). "Meek" is probably not the best word to use
here according to some scholars. The Hebrew word
used in the Old Testament (Psalm 37) underlying this
text is *anawim.* The *anawim* shall inherit the earth:
the people who suffer tribulation, distress, persecution, famine, nakedness, peril and the sword: the
people who appear, in this present age, least likely to
inherit the earth.

The dispossessed celebrate this promise,
proclaiming with Mary that the same promise made
also to Abraham is now fulfilled (Lk 1:55). Faith
makes the difference. Gloom and defeatism are
dispelled.

God had promised victory. Jesus is "the *Yes* to all
of God's promises" (2 Cor 1:20). In him, the dispossessed recognize themselves as conquerors.

Sarah

SARAH, a poor woman from the
squatters' village, walked into our agency one day, sat
down in the chair next to my desk and began to tell me
about her life. I listened to her problems and request.
I made a quick mental review of the different
categories of assistance which our agency provides
and realized that her petition did not fit into any of

our categories or programs. I told her that we did not deal with what she required. Then I suggested a few other agencies where she might get that form of assistance. It was all very clean and professional. But Sarah did not play her part. She was supposed to say thank you, and leave. Instead, she just sat there. I tapped my fingers on the desk. Then I cleared my throat (harumph). Still she sat there. I stood up, shook her hand with my right one, and pointed to the door with my left. She wouldn't budge. She wouldn't even release my hand. I was beginning to feel annoyed. Finally, I shook my hand free, and told her that she had to go. She refused, and bluntly replied that she was not budging until I helped her. And so we played a waiting game.

I pretended to do desk work, looking up now and then to see if she was getting tired. She sat there like a rock. What was I going to do? I had reviewed all our programs and she didn't fit any of them. Her case was rejected. We had a whole file of rejected cases. Why couldn't she accept that?

That day I realized that even our wonderful service agency for the poor was a fallen creature, just like other fallen institutions. And that we, too, would make people feel rejected, misfit.

The beauty about Sarah is that she refused our easy categorization of her. She did not fall prey to the seduction of poverty. She wouldn't accept the status of a rejected case nor would she be brushed off and dismissed. In fact, what she finally did was grab a broom, started sweeping, and got herself hired as the cleaning lady for the agency. Jesus once encountered a woman much like Sarah. Her story is found in the Gospel of Matthew.

> As they were going, a woman who had suffered
> from hemorrhages for twelve years came up
> behind him and touched the tassel of his cloak.
> "If only I can touch his cloak," she thought, "I
> shall get well." Jesus turned around and saw her
> and said, "Take courage, daughter! Your faith
> has restored your health." That very moment the
> woman got well.   (Mt 9:20-22)

In the time and culture of Jesus men did not associate much with women in public. It was considered unclean. Similarly, it was unclean to put oneself in contact with blood.

The woman with the hemorrhage, therefore, had two strikes against her which made her an untouchable, a misfit, a rejected case.

Approaching and touching him, this woman demonstrated a certain fearlessness. She would not accept the verdict that society had passed on her. Her boldness indicated an interior freedom, a refusal to accept the demeaning definition imposed on her.

Jesus responded to her intrepid determination with warm hospitality: he let her touch him. She was accepted and healed.

Jesus understood the feelings of people whom society rejects. He, too, as son of Mary, had experienced being socially outcast (some neighbors might well have considered him a bastard had they suspected his fatherless origin). He, too, as son of a dispossessed woman, had experienced the stigmatization of poverty.

The words of Jesus to this woman show his understanding of her feelings. He affirmed the bravery she had already displayed. And then called her to greater boldness: "Take courage, daughter!"

To all the marginalized, Jesus says, "Take courage!" He calls them to refuse the lie imposed on them by the Master Deceiver. They are not untouchable. Jesus Christ has touched them. They are not marginal. They stand at the center of his new creation.

Jesus would tell every outcast, "Take courage!" Reject the lie. You have been accepted!" Indeed, God has "lifted up the lowly," "has kept the promise" and "has remembered to show mercy" (Lk 1:52, 54, 55).

7

SINGING
THE HOSPITALITY
OF REFUGEES

"He has filled the hungry with
good things." (Lk 1:53)

Ibrahim And Oz

In January, 1982, I received a
long distance phone call from the United States. It
was about seven in the morning Nairobi time, eleven
at night in New York. I heard my father's voice. The
tone of the first few words of greeting prepared me
for the worst. Then he said, "We have some bad
news." I braced myself. "Grandma has passed away."
I don't remember what he said after that.

I left the telephone and made a beeline for my
bedroom. I wanted to be alone. I certainly didn't want

57

anyone to see me or the expression on my face. But I was followed.

Once in my own room the tears came. I just stood there, alone, sobbing. Then Ibrahim walked through the door.

Ibrahim was a young man from Eritrea, a part of northern Ethiopia. He had been living with us for several months while waiting to emigrate to Canada. Several members of his immediate family had been killed in the long civil war between Eritrea and Ethiopia.

Ibrahim looked straight at me and said two simple words: "I understand." He held me and we wept together.

Ibrahim was *our* guest, but I learned a lot from him about hospitality. He helped me at that moment when I was asking the hard questions, the value questions: Why was I in Africa? What was it worth? All I wanted was to be back home.

Ibrahim had asked those questions himself and he knew the feeling. Without saying anything more than "I understand," he made me feel at home. He widened my experience of what home means. A shared grief made us brothers.

It was not only me whom Ibrahim helped. Though a guest of our community, he made us all feel welcome in our own house. He was always available. He worked at various domestic jobs like washing dishes, sweeping the floor, setting the table, clearing the yard. He was always cheerful and found ways to make us laugh. He even mediated conflicts. When he finally found a sponsor and left our community to go to Canada, we felt as if the host of the party was leaving the guests. At the end of that year with

Ibrahim, we were the ones who experienced the meaning of "coming home."

When I reflect on how Ibrahim changed our community, I am reminded of Dorothy in *The Wizard of Oz*. The analogy is a bit silly perhaps, except that Dorothy, too, created a community while a refugee in a foreign land.

She decides to walk the yellow brick road to the city of Oz, where the great Wizard lives. She thinks that he can bring her home. Along the road, she meets three sojourners: the brainless Scarecrow, the heartless Tin Man, and the cowardly Lion. She forms this motley band into a travelling community. She, an exile in *their* land, makes them feel at home.

Each of these characters has big expectations of the Wizard. They are given a task, however, which requires different feats of cunning, compassion, and courage. They accomplish the task, happy and surprised by personal resources they had never tapped.

When they return to the city of Oz, the great Wizard tells them that he has nothing to give them. He has no magic powers. In that instant, the Scarecrow realizes that there is nothing magical about thinking; he discovers that he always had a brain. The Tin Man realizes there is nothing magical about feeling; that he always had a heart. The Lion realizes there is nothing magical about courage; that he always had a will. They are each enriched by their new self-image. Dorothy, too, realizes there is nothing magical about going home: she discovers that home is as near as clicking her heels.

The "Oz experience" is like diving from a high cliff into the sea of one's own inner potential. It is discovering that one always possessed the powers one was seeking whether it be a brain, a heart or courage. The Oz experience is coming home to oneself.

Ibrahim taught me that hospitality is the ministry of empowerment. We cannot wave a magic wand to make vanish the miseries of those we serve. What we can do is reveal to others their ability to solve their own problems. We can challenge sojourners to grow by applying their hidden gifts to reach their destination.

This is what Ibrahim did for us. He was displaced but quite comfortable in Oz. He showed us how not to be afraid of the yellow brick road, the unknown twisting path of life. When the time came for him to go, the individuals in our house found themselves woven together in new fraternal bonds. We had become a better community, which discovered, indeed, that it had a brain, a heart, and a bit more courage.

Resurrection
And Hospitality

IN JANUARY, 1983, I was passing through Nigeria. The government had just issued an order expelling two million Ghanaians, some of whom had been living in Nigeria for decades. I saw families carrying their mattresses, bedding, pots and pans, clothes and sundry boxes full of odds and ends. A few people died on the trek through Benin and Togo. The others faced a very hard life back in Ghana, still in the throes of its long economic decline.

During that same year there was heated debate in the U.S. Congress about lowering the country's global quota for the number of refugees it would receive. The quota for Africa, in fact, had always been low. In spite of the millions of African refugees, the quota for that continent is one of the most restricted. Only a few thousand annually are permitted entry into the United States.

Hospitality has often been cited as characteristic of the Risen Christ. In the Gospel of John (21:9-13), the disciples find Jesus at the water's edge preparing a breakfast of fish and bread over a charcoal fire. Jesus tells them to bring along a few of the one hundred fifty three fish they had just miraculously caught. Inviting them to "come and eat," he shared this simple meal with them and they recognized him as the Lord. The same recognition of the Lord takes place in the Gospel of Luke (24:30-31) when Jesus breaks bread at the table with two disciples he had joined on the walk to Emmaus. In both instances, Christ is revealed in an act of hospitality.

The early Church, similarly, shared in the life of her Risen Lord through hospitality: by having "their meals together in their home, eating food with glad and humble hearts" (Ac 2:46), and "sharing their belongings with those in need" (Ac 4:32-35).

The Church continues to manifest the power of the Resurrection by her attempt to find homes for the millions of displaced persons in the world. Parishes and individuals have sponsored refugees from such diverse places as Ethiopia, Somalia, Vietnam, Laos, Cambodia, El Salvador, Haiti and other troubled areas. By making arrangements through local offices of Catholic charities, sponsors and refugees have been brought together for a mutually enriching experience. These sponsors have strengthened the local Church's witness to the risen Lord by their hospitality. Their action points to Jesus who stood on the shore to receive those whose dreams had likewise been shattered.

How is it possible? The answer to this question is found on the gibbet of the cross. There, by totally emptying himself (the *kenosis* of Ph 2:6-11), Jesus opened his heart and made room for all in his Body, the Church, represented by Mary. The disciple John, at the foot of the cross, and all future generations in every part of the world are received into his family: "Behold your son" (Jn 19:26).

When Jesus emptied himself, his open body became the Church, the family of Mary.

It is in self-emptying that persons from different cultures are able to receive and accept each other. This is the lesson African refugees have taught me. When, as an American, I am too full of my own culture and worried too much about my own "identity," then there is no room for anyone who threatens these. But when I am able to open myself to a stranger and say, "Friend, behold your brother," then I re-enact the last words of Jesus, and share in the *kenosis* which leads to Easter.

I have heard some people in the U.S. say, "There is no more room." Especially during these times of economic pinch we are less inclined to offer hospitality and risk the cross of self-emptying. The disciples, too, feared this cross. Being received by the Lord is what made them able to receive others.

Jesus stood on the shore shouting to a group of hungry and discouraged fishermen to cast out their nets again. To prove to them their own capabilities, he had the nets filled to the brim with one hundred fifty three fish. This number is significant: one hundred fifty three, according to some scholars, was the number of known "nationalities" on earth at that time. John makes a final observation about the net which represents the resourcefulness of the Church: "Even though there were so many, still the net did not tear" (Jn 21:11). Christian hospitality, then, receives many and does not tear. It is a beautiful and clear witness of our faith in the Risen Lord.

Galut

"By faith Abraham obeyed the call to go out to a land destined for himself and his heirs, to leave home without knowing where he was to go" (Heb 11:8).

REFUGEES are dreamers. The Bible was in large part written by this kind of dreamer: people longing to reach the promised land or return to it from exile. Commenting on the Jewish experience of life, Rita Gross says in *Woman Spirit Rising*, "The most profound, intriguing and inviting of Jewish theologies, the Kabalah, teaches us that *galut* or exile is the fundamental reality and pain of present existence."

This *galut* burns inside refugees. They are displaced people: out of an old place and not yet in a new one. They are neither home, nor are they yet settled in a promised land. They are in an in-between place both physically and psychologically. This displacement, halfway from an old reality and halfway to a new one, can create passion.

People with *galut* are capable of great vision. Some are poets and fighters. Often they see farther than others into the promised land, for their eyes are trained in the practice of hope. They strain harder to hear the whisper of angels. They lean a bit more over the rail which separates this world from the Kingdom. Some lean so far over the rail that they slip and plunge headlong into God.

Those who experience exile are faced with two fundamental choices: remain homeless or make a home in the "not yet." Those who choose the first option take a smaller risk and lead a sort of life in the halfway place. Those who choose the second option are not satisfied with the in-between. They dare to lean over the rail. They dare to live as if they had already arrived in the promised land. They make a home of the future.

In 1986 on the evening of January 7th, the day Coptic Christians commemorate the Lord's nativity, the Marianists were invited to join a few hundred Ethiopian refugees to celebrate Christmas. It took place in a rented hall. There was Injera, the staple food of Ethiopia, with a sauce of eggs and meat. There were posters with holiday greetings in Amharic. There were streamers and other decorations. There were a few people dressed in festive traditional costume. Most of all, there was good cheer.

The highlight of the evening was the singing of Ethiopian Christmas Carols. Judging from the reaction of that receptive audience, there were both funny and serious songs included in the evening's program. One particular song, however, drew the most enthusiastic response.

An old man got up on the stage. He was dressed in a traditional sort of tunic. He said that he was going to sing a song entitled *"Tarikin Betarick Geta Yiseral,"* which, he explained, in English means "history will be changed by History."

The old man began singing while beating on a shoulder drum. The combination of his voice and the drum created rhythmic waves which seemed to caress the crowd which was as quiet as a beach lapped by a timeless sea. Now and then the sadness in his voice changed. The volume and conviction of his voice increased in such a way that it seemed to bubble like a fountain. At these intervals in the song he also raised his eyes to the ceiling and threw back his head. I was wondering if at this point he was singing the refraining title.

When the song ended, the old man stepped down from the stage. The room full of festive young people was absolutely still, until finally one by one they began to applaud. I got up from my chair and followed the old man outside the hall. When I caught up to him on the patio where we were engulfed by the dark night, I asked him to tell me what he meant by "history will be changed by History."

He told me, "Caesar Augustus, the all powerful Emperor and the ruler of the colony of Israel, ordered a census. He did it for his own purposes, for manipulating and controlling a colonized people. Caesar

Augustus was making history, that sad history of wars, and persecutions, exile and oppression. At the very same time" — and the old man's eyes grew wide — "God was using these evil forces for his own Divine purpose. Even in the forced movement of his family from Nazareth to Bethlehem, even when his people were most brutalized, the Christ Child was transforming all these unhappy events to bring about God's justice." The old man paused and said, "history will be changed by History." Then we listened to the night, each with our own thoughts.

Many things went through my mind. I thought again of the Master Deceiver and how he would have us assume the worst conclusion for every sad piece of history. And I thought of Mary who did *not* assume the worst, even when the evidence gave her every reason to do so. This expecting mother. Expecting abundance even when her people were being impoverished by a colonial exploiter. Expecting light even in that epoch of confusion and darkness. Expecting the Messiah and his Kingdom even when her people were most afflicted and in bondage. I imagined how Mary's faith and the faith of this old man must infuriate the Master Deceiver.

The old man began to speak again and told me that the refrain of that Christmas song concludes with the words *Birhanun Yawetal Kibru Yigeletal,* which he said, in English means "He will let the light shine and his glory shall be manifested."

"After the birth of Jesus Christ," the old man went on, "the kind of history Caesar Augustus makes, the same kind which we refugees suffer, is like a candle flame in the sunshine." He said that people without faith are hypnotized by the candle flame of

Caesar's history. They stare at this seducing sign, worry anxiously and even despair. Those with faith, however, see the candle burning but are not deceived or frightened by it. Instead, they note how the candle flicker, compared to the brilliance of the rising sun, is relatively insignificant. "The people who walked in darkness have seen a great light" (Isaiah 9:2). Caesar's history, "The boots of the invading army and all their bloodstained clothing" (Is 9:5), is changed by God's History, "A child born to us . . . our ruler . . . the Prince of Peace" (Is 9:6).

The light of God's History is perceived by hearts straining with the passion of *galut*, by refugees who choose to become pilgrims. Yes,

> history will be changed by History
> He will let the light shine and
> His glory shall be manifested.

8

MIRROR
OF REDEMPTION

"My soul magnifies the Lord"
(Lk 1:46)

Stabat Mater
(Standing Mother)

THERE IS a message for us in the person of Mary at the foot of the cross. She bravely stands there as Jesus hangs in torment. She stands beside Jesus as others have stood beside those unjustly persecuted. She is visible in others who have taken a stand for the oppressed, others such as Oscar Romero, Martin Luther King, Steve Biko, Jerzy Popieluszko. Like Mary these witnesses of conscience have stood beside the powerless: there, with her, they have stood against systems of injustice, against "the pricipalities and powers.

69

At the foot of the cross, Mary was standing up against all that brings down the poor. She stood on Calvary's hill as a witness, a lone witness. She stood in protest. That is how she shared in the exaltation of her son in his hour. She did not cower, she did not run, she did not excuse, she did not compromise with injustice. She *pointed* to it as she stood at the foot of the cross.

The fortitude of Mary, standing *beside* the outcast and standing *against* the "mighty on their thrones," is humble courage. It risks everything for love. The way she stood beside her condemned son is the way hundreds and thousands of people today stand beside the oppressed. She stood. They, perhaps, march. But the purpose is the same: not to run, not to cower, not to excuse, rather to point to injustice. To point by standing.

The Face Of God

ONE LENT a couple of years ago I was attending the Way of the Cross at a small mission outstation in Tanzania. The first thing I should mention about this service is that it was in Swahili. This is significant because of the shade of meaning that Swahili gives to the expression, "My child died." On the occasion of such a tragedy one might hear, "*Nimefiwa na mtoto wangu*," or "I am died to by my child." This way of expressing the loss of a child in the passive voice illustrates how African parents experience themselves not only as bereaved people but as co-victims of that son or daughter's death.

About sixty people were led in the meditation by three altar boys who went from station to station with cross, candles and missal. The actual pictures depicting the passion were thinly streaked with water marks from last year's rainy season. There were no chairs and so the congregation knelt together in little groups on the cement floor. What struck me most was the reality of this experience for the people. They were being "died to by Jesus." They were moved to emotion-filled clapping and wailing.

At about the fourth station, I noticed the woman next to me was facing the wrong way, in the opposite direction of the station. In fact, she was face to face with me. I looked directly at her and realized that she was blind. I couldn't help but stare at this woman's face. She was elderly but spritely, with a sharply focused expression. Her spare black hair, streaked with white, was matted beneath an old printed kerchief commemorating Tanzania's Independence Day. She had strong and resilient facial features. One would suppose her to be a powerful matriarch of a large extended family. But at this moment her forehead was quite wrinkled. Her lips were slack from inaudible prayers which she continuously mumbled without the aid of too many teeth. She kept shaking her head, would pause, and hold her head up high. What personal tragedies were being relived behind those sightless eyes, I don't know. As she sang out the plaintive songs of crucifixion, she might well have been reliving the death of one of her own; perhaps a son or daughter. Whatever she was thinking, love was reflected in every line of her face. And the light within her was shining.

As I thought about that woman at various times that Lent, the significance of Mary at the foot of the cross slowly dawned on me.

It can be said that Mary's presence at Calvary was a terrible suffering for Jesus. But I wonder.

To express the paradox of filial trust in the midst of apparent paternal neglect, Jesus utters the first line of Psalm 22: "My God, my God, why have you forsaken me?" We are familiar with the vivid description of desolation in this Psalm, and yet, if those at the foot of the cross prayed it to the conclusion, this Psalm would have surprised them with its tone of unexpected triumph.

> Then I shall proclaim your name to my brothers.
> Praise you in full assembly:
> You who fear Yahweh, praise Him!
> Entire race of Jacob, glorify Him!
> Entire race of Israel, revere Him!
>
> For He has not despised
> or disdained the poor man in his poverty,
> has not hidden His face from him,
> but has answered him when he called. . . .
>
> The whole earth, from end to end,
>   will remember
> and come back to Yahweh. . . .

I think the turning point of this Psalm, and a vital image of Mary's role at the foot of the cross, is:

"(Yahweh) has not hidden His face from him. . ."

How is it — as Jesus implies — that the face of God is not hidden from him? After all, he has been betrayed by a friend. He has been tortured and ridiculed by his enemies. He has been completely abandoned by his followers. And now he is hanging on a gibbet outside the city walls in the place of the skull: rejected and deserted. How can he say that the face of God is not hidden from him?

If she looks anything like that old Tanzanian woman, I think Jesus finds immense comfort in gazing upon Mary at the foot of the cross. Her face had always communicated tenderness and hope. Though now her brow be wrinkled and her hair be white, she looks upon him with matronly courage, and exudes an indomitable faith. In her bright eyes, the darkness of Golgotha is pierced. The light within her shines on Jesus. Could hers be the unhidden face of God?

The Face Of Redeemed Humanity

ON THE CROSS Jesus had a final temptation. The Master Deceiver whispered in his ear: "Humanity is irredeemable." As a dying man, Jesus was subject to that greatest of all temptations: despair. Why did he not give up? What was the consciousness of Jesus at that grim moment?

His mind, dulled by pain, was focused on something beyond his pain. According to Biblical scholars, the crucifixion portrayal of St. John reveals the consciousness of Jesus as triumphant. He had anticipated being "raised up" on the cross, and he considered it the signal of his victory. In spite of the suffering, and over against the temptation to despair, Jesus focused his attention upon the fruit of his passion. In Mary, Jesus was gazing upon redeemed humanity.

Mary is the dawn of the Parousia. The crucified one saw in her the treasure for which he was paying the price. He saw millions of dispossessed (*Stabat Pauper*) standing in possession. He saw millions of refugees (*Stabat Exsul*) standing at home. He saw millions of oppressed people (*Stabat Libertus*) standing liberated. He saw you and me, as we will be someday, standing in the glory of our risen bodies.

In Mary, Jesus saw the new humanity for which he was dying. He could gaze through her, as through a window, to see the working of the Father, the Potter at His wheel, molding the future shape of human experience. She was then, as always, the woman of promise; the mirror of redemption.

Jesus did not believe the big lie. In spite of the inhumanity of his death, he did not see inhuman people at the foot of the cross. Each and every face at the foot of the cross — and throughout history — rather looked to him like the face of that old Tanzanian Mama, like the face of Mary, the face of redeemed humanity, the unhidden face of God.

Pietà

THERE ARE two postures Mary assumes in relation to Jesus, one standing and one sitting. As Stabat Mater, she stands beside those who are suffering and tempted to despair. As Pietà, she cradles the dead.

Jesus reveals at this hour the way he experiences death. He quotes Psalm 22 to express his attitude toward apparent divine desertion. This Psalm, as we have seen, describes all the agony of crucifixion. It also images this agony as a birth and God as a midwife.

Yet you drew me out of the womb,
You entrusted me to my mother's breasts;
placed me on your lap from my birth,
from my mother's womb you have been my God.

(Ps 22:9-10)

On the cross, a New Humanity is born. This same instrument of execution becomes the birthing table. Death is the passageway for the Risen One, delivered by the midwifery of God.

The Pietà is not a biblical image. It springs from the imagination of Christian artists who have tried to portray Jesus' understanding of death. When Jesus says, "Into your hands I commend my spirit," we might image death having maternal arms.

The human imagination dishes up many symbols for death. There is death the reaper with scythe in hand. There is death the hour glass almost empty. There is death the skull and crossed bones. Unaided by revelation, the human mind seldom images death as anything but awful.

The Pietà is different. Death is presented as mother. In Michelangelo's work, this mother is tender beyond telling. She is at peace with eyes closed, but her whole body is attentive to the one she receives. Her legs are steady to make a soft lap for the broken one. Her arm is attentive, and mighty to hold him from slipping. Indeed, what powerful arms. Such arms could hold all humanity without one person slipping away.

In Africa I have seen too many children die. I can't stop thinking about them, remembering their names, recalling their faces. I question their senseless dying. Sometimes it is too much for me, and I am tempted to believe the lie of futility.

The Pietà does not stop such questioning. To be human is to ask such questions. The Pietà, however, does symbolize our faith that these children have simply gone home early. She symbolizes our faith that death is a tender mother receiving us, and carrying us into the Parousia with mighty arms.

The Pietà is a Christian image very similar to the Jewish image of the bosom of Abraham. This large lap and soft bosom cradle us at death. We are safely enclosed on all sides. There is no slipping away. The spiritual about Abraham's bosom could also be sung about the lap of Mary.

> So high you can't get over it,
> so low you can't get under it,
> so wide you can't get round it,
> Oh, bless my soul.

The Pietà is a stone mirror of Redemption: the transformation of death; a new freedom for people oppressed by the lie, "who through fear of death were subject to slavery all their lives" (Heb 2:15).

Mirror
Of Redeemed Humanity

WHY IS Mary an Icon of courage?
In the preceding chapters Mary has been depicted as
standing among the dispossessed as promise, and
standing among refugees as host. She is able to stand
so, sharing the life of the poor and the rejected,
because she believed. This is why she was, for Jesus, a
symbol, an image, a mentor in courage. In so far as I
become Christlike I enter into his relationships and so
Mary becomes for me, as well, a model in courage.

How is Mary the mirror of Redemption? In the
preceding chapters Mary's role as mirror of Redemption is described by the words "promise" and "host."
In the language of mystery this could be expressed by
the titles of the Immaculate Conception and the
Assumption.

As the Immaculate Conception, Mary fulfilled
the promise made to Eve that the head of the serpent
would be crushed, that evil would be overcome. As
the first to be redeemed and made whole by Jesus
Christ, she personifies the promise tenaciously held
by the dispossessed. As the Immaculate Conception,
Mary is a mirror that reflects to us our redeemed
humanity, our victory, our true worth.

As the Assumption, Mary plays host to
humankind longing to come home to God. She invites
us now to enter into the "not yet," into God's future,
the Kingdom. Mary of the Assumption personifies
the hospitality of the refugee mother who serves at
the wedding banquet prepared by Jesus Christ. As the
Assumption, Mary is a mirror that reflects to us our

redeemed humanity, our homecoming, our acceptance by God.

Why do we need this mirror of Redemption? Most reflections we have of ourselves are disheartening. People, left to themselves, are often deceived by that diabolical mirror which distorts their beauty, which tempts them with self-hatred. This diabolical mirror is the main tool of all oppression.

How does our reflection in the mirror of Redemption give us courage? The person of Mary unveils the gratuitous consummation of the human project. We see what we are becoming. We are spellbound by this lovely image. We stare at ourselves not believing we are so beautiful, though God has been trying for centuries to convince us of this. Dostoievsky described this Divine activity when he said, "The world will be saved by beauty."

The central message of this little book is that Jesus Christ lifts up the lowly and feeds the hungry. He exposes the lie which keeps us dispossessed and exiled. This lie, the main tool of all oppression, expressed in such words as "unable" and "unworthy," is proven bogus by God's empowering love revealed in Jesus Christ, our Redeemer.

The model disciple, Mary, mirrors this fact of Redemption in her fearless song and courageous life. She is Christlike. She is promise to the dispossessed and hospitality to the rejected.

The words of Ecclesiastes 8:1 could be applied to such a believer: "The wisdom of a person lends brightness to her face; her face, once grim, is altered." A believer's face is not placid with the sagging gloom of the cynic. The face of the believer, rather, mirrors the surging gladness of God.

Each and every Christian disciple, then, is called like Mary to mirror the redemption, to smash the diabolical image which frightens and enslaves humanity, to be models and mentors in courage.

Christ's disciple is one who sings the Magnificat, the song of faith. He or she sings of the Kingdom at a time when the living conditions of God's people are anything but the Kingdom, when these conditions are oppressive and the people are lured by the lie of the Master Deceiver to wallow in defeat.

Christ's disciple is one who stands at the foot of many crosses: who stands beside the poor, who stands beside the refugees, who stands beside those tempted to give up, and mirrors Redemption. Standing is the posture of indomitable faith which we can learn from Mary, our sister sojourner and our Stabat Mater.

> Sister, hold my hand
> together let's walk
> unafraid, stepping
> bold into tomorrow.
>
> Sister, point there
> when my eyes grow dim;
> push me when my heart
> grows tepid and trembles.
>
> Sister, tell me of Him
> when the din so loud
> speaks other names, and
> lures me away from Zion.
>
> Sister, pray with me
> when I most want to turn
> around and run from
> His voice calling.

To greater freedom
to greater justice
to greater love
to the new earth.

Sister, let me sing
with you on that Day
of the hungry fed,
the poor lifted up.

Maranatha! Come, Lord Jesus!
Maranatha! Maranatha!   Amen.